May 2019

spot

BABY FARM ANIMALS

PUPPIES

by Anastasia Suen

AMICUS | AMICUS INK

ear

eye

Look for these
words and pictures
as you read.

nose

paw

Have you ever seen a puppy?
A puppy is a baby dog.

A mother has many puppies. For two weeks, they eat and sleep all day. They grow.

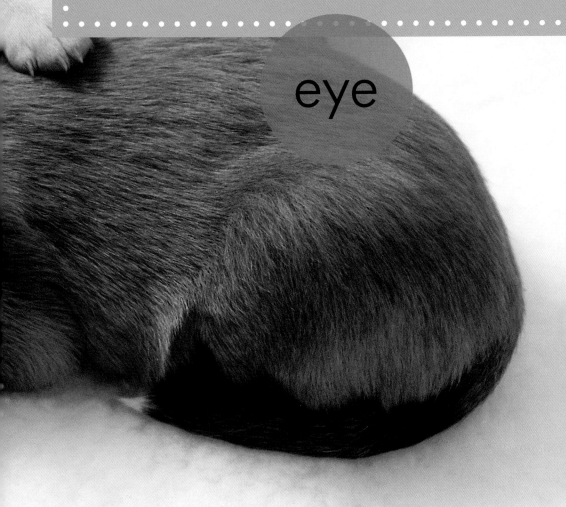

Look at the puppy's eyes.
They will not open for ten days.

eye

Look at the puppy's paw.
It has claws.
It has five pads.

paw

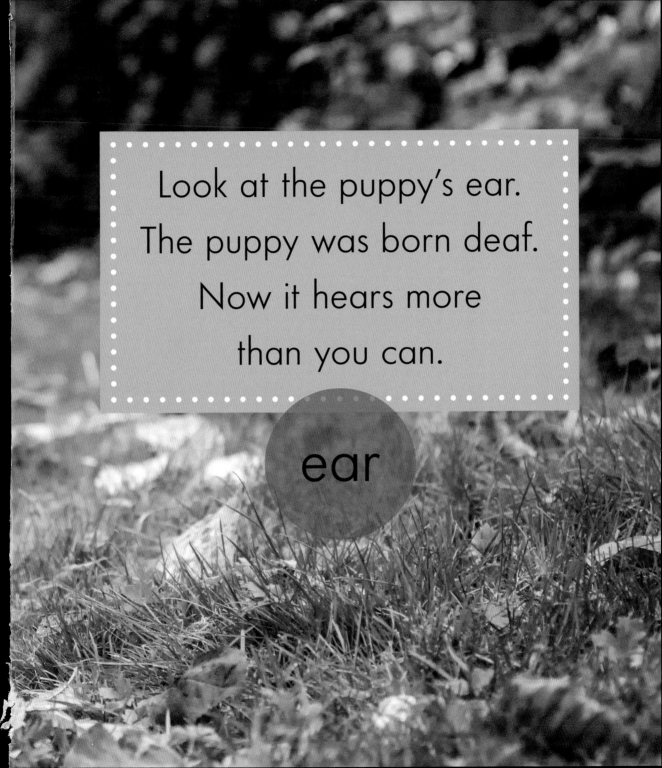

Look at the puppy's ear.
The puppy was born deaf.
Now it hears more
than you can.

ear

Look at the puppy's nose.
It can smell more
than yours can.

nose

A puppy will grow up.
It will learn to work.
It will keep sheep together.

ear

eye

Did you find?

nose

paw

spot

Spot is published by Amicus and Amicus Ink
P.O. Box 1329, Mankato, MN 56002
www.amicuspublishing.us

Library of Congress Cataloging-in-Publication Data
Names: Suen, Anastasia, author.
Title: Puppies / by Anastasia Suen.
Description: Mankato, MN : Amicus, [2019] | Series: Spot
 baby farm animals
Identifiers: LCCN 2017055786 (print) | LCCN 2017056539
 (ebook) | ISBN 9781681515731 (pdf) | ISBN 9781681515359
 (library binding) | ISBN 9781681523736 (pbk.)
Subjects: LCSH: Puppies--Juvenile literature.
Classification: LCC SF426.5 (ebook) | LCC SF426.5 .S842 2019
 (print) | DDC 636.7/07--dc23
LC record available at https://lccn.loc.gov/2017055786

Printed in China

HC 10 9 8 7 6 5 4 3 2 1
PB 10 9 8 7 6 5 4 3 2 1

Wendy Dieker and
 Mary Ellen Klukow, editors
Deb Miner, series designer
Aubrey Harper, book designer
Holly Young, photo researcher

Photos by Shutterstock/ksana2010
cover, Getty/Jane Burton, 6–7,
Grigorita Ko 8–9, eAlisa 14;
iStock/Eriklam 1, JLSnader 3,
GlobalP 4–5, MirasWonderland
12–13; Alamy/Janet Horton, 10-11

PUPPIES